I0554629

MASTER
SIN

—— OR ——

SIN WILL MASTER YOU

W. RUTH TURNER, P.E.

Paperback ISBN 978-1-960007-20-9
eBook ISBN 978-1-960007-21-6

Published by
Mercy & Moxie
An Imprint of
Orison Publishers, Inc.
PO Box 188, Grantham, PA 17027
www.OrisonPublishers.com

Dedication

To my mother, Ms. Willie Jewel Johnson, who encouraged me to get the message of *Master Sin or Sin Will Master You* out to the world. I appreciate you for being the constant reminder of the weight and gravity of its truth and impact for everyday living and eternal life. May you be richly rewarded for your prayers and role in its release and lives being changed, communities healed and the Kingdom of God expanded.

Contents

Introduction

Our battle with sin is real, and Paul, the apostle, recognized it. He voiced the frustration we feel in our struggle and the hope and victory we find in Jesus Christ.

I've tried everything, and nothing helps. I'm at the end of my rope. Is there no one who can do anything for me? Isn't that the real question?

The answer, thank God, is that Jesus Christ can and does. He acted to set things right in this life of contradictions where I want to serve God with all my heart and mind, but am *pulled by the influence of sin* to do something totally different (Romans 7:24–25 MSG, italics mine).

This sin struggle affects all of us. As Paul said, "...*all have sinned* and fall short of the glory of God" (Romans 3:23 NASB, italics mine).

What can we do about it? If we all sin and none of us can really overcome this problem on our own, then why fight it?

What is the use? Is it really as bad as some people say?

Paul told one group of early Christians with obvious sin problems, "I discipline my body like an athlete, training it to do what it should. Otherwise, I fear that after preaching to others I myself might be disqualified" (1 Corinthians 9:27 NLT). *Sin is the opponent; therefore, it must be mastered or it will master you.*

Jesus Christ gives us the power we need to overcome sin, but you and I must learn to do as Paul did and train ourselves to live and do as we should.

Read on to discover how you can master sin, overcome temptations and conquer the desires of the flesh through the Word of God and power of the Holy Spirit.

Chapter One

Sin and Its Impact

I f I've learned anything in my life as a believer and minister, it is that responsibility for my choices does not end at the altar. The Bible explains it best:

> First to those in Damascus, then to those in Jerusalem and in all Judea, and then to the Gentiles, I preached that they should repent and turn to God *and demonstrate their repentance by their deeds* (Acts 26:20 NIV, italics mine).

Our deeds or actions don't save us, but they do demonstrate or offer proof that we have been saved and are being transformed. In other words, you and I have to do more than "talk the walk." We have to *walk the walk* with Jesus. We are not perfect, but we are *being perfected*. It won't happen if we fail to do our part in walking with God.

We have no chance of mastering or overcoming "sin" if we don't understand what it really is. The *Merriam-Webster Dictionary* defines sin in the following way:

1

1a: an offense against religious or moral law
  b: an action that is or is felt to be highly reprehensible "it's a *sin* to waste food"
  c: an often serious shortcoming: FAULT
2a: transgression of the law of God...[1]

The apostle John categorized sin under three headings: the lust of the flesh, the lust of the eye and the pride of life (see 1 John 2:16).

The Book of Proverbs frames sin as seven things that God "hates" or that are "an abomination" to Him (Proverbs 6:16–19 MEV):

1. A proud look
2. A lying tongue
3. Hands that shed innocent blood
4. A heart that devises wicked imaginations
5. Feet that are swift in running to mischief
6. A false witness who speaks lies
7. He who sows discord among brethren

The apostle Paul describes seventeen kinds of sin (or "works of the flesh") in the Book of Galatians:

Now the works of the flesh are revealed, which are these: adultery, sexual immorality, impurity, lewdness, idolatry, sorcery, hatred, strife, jealousy, rage, selfishness, dissensions, heresies, envy, murders, drunkenness, carousing, and the like. I warn you, as I previously warned you, that those who do such things shall not inherit the kingdom of God (Galatians 5:19–21 MEV).

Both the Old and the New Testaments of the Bible warn

us that if we do these things, then we are not ready for heaven. To have eternal life, each of us must repent of and turn away from our sin and receive Jesus Christ as our Savior and Lord. Then we must adopt a new lifestyle centered on the Word of God.

Sin isn't merely something we hope we don't get caught doing. Sin is destructive, even if we never get "caught" in it. When we give in and surrender to it, sin can bring shame, injury, devastation or loss, especially of one's soul.

On a deeper level, when we disobey God's Word, we become violators or transgressors of His Word and we breach or violate our relationship with God and one another. This brings destructive consequences to any individual, family or society.

The Reality

As an African American, I am especially concerned about the national crime statistics that reveal the shockingly high number of black-on-black crimes recorded each year. I also understand and relate to those who suffer from racism and inequities in the world. I've faced my own challenges as a black woman in the workplace, in public service, in business and even in ministry. However, while we may not have control over the racial views of others, we do have the power to make our own choices and can choose our actions in life.

Poverty can lead you to feel as if you were born to be a victim for life, or it can become the fuel to power your drive out of poverty and into a life of joy, accomplishment and perpetual giving to others.

The world is filled with incredible stories of children from different races who were born poor but who managed to earn doctorate degrees, found businesses and transform communities as adults. In virtually every case, these overcomers made choices and took actions to change the direction of their lives. They took control of the sad narratives of their childhood and rewrote their story to match the desires of their hearts.

Sadly, many who grow up under difficult or unfair circumstances allow excuses and bad choices to become driving forces in their lives. Even worse, innocent victims or families often suffer as a result of those choices.

We will begin our discussion of sin with an examination of the first recorded homicide in the Bible in the next chapter. But first, let's examine some relatively new federal statistics on homicides in the United States. According to the U.S. Department of Justice-Federal Bureau of Investigation report titled, "2019 Crime in the United States":

- In 2019, most (78.3 percent) of the 13,927 murder victims for whom supplemental data was received were male. (Based on *Expanded Homicide Data Table 1*.)
- Of the murder victims for whom race was known, 54.7 percent were Black or African American, 42.3 percent were White, and 3.1 percent were of other races. Race was unknown for 234 victims. (Based on *Expanded Homicide Data Table 2*.)
- Of the offenders for whom gender was known, 88.0 percent were male. (Based on *Expanded Homicide Data Table 3*.)
- When the race of the offender was known, 55.9 percent were Black or African American, 41.1 percent were White, and 3.0 percent were of other races. The race was unknown for 4,752 offenders. (Based on *Expanded Homicide Data Table 3*.)[2]

The same report also noted that of the 2019 homicides for which supplementary homicide data was received, 1,810 victims (13.0 percent) were slain by family members; 1,372 victims (9.9 percent) were murdered by strangers; and 3,937 victims (28.3

4

percent) were slain by "other known" offenders. The offenders were not known for 6,808 murder victims (48.9 percent).[3]

The report also noted that 85 husbands were killed by their wives, 482 wives were slain by their husbands, 166 mothers were murdered by their children, 178 fathers were killed by their children, 259 sons were slain by their parents, 171 daughters were murdered by their parents, 115 brothers were killed by their siblings, 27 sisters were slain by their siblings, and 327 victims were murdered by other family members.[4]

Of the 3,937 victims known to have been killed by someone outside their family in 2019, 2,773 victims were killed by acquaintances, 345 were slain by friends, 187 boyfriends were murdered by their girlfriends, 505 girlfriends were killed by their boyfriends, and 100 victims were slain by their neighbors.[5]

In a sad echo of the first homicide in the Bible, the FBI report said where the circumstances were known about the homicides, 43.2 percent of the victims were murdered *during arguments.*[6]

Anger left unchecked leads to sin, which adversely affects individuals, families and nations. It can bring destruction to you and everyone connected to you.

Review again Apostle Paul's words to Roman believers. They echo the frustration many of us experience in life:

I've tried everything and nothing helps. I'm at the end of my rope. Is there no one who can do anything for me? Isn't that the real question?

The answer, thank God, is that Jesus Christ can and does. He acted to set things right in this life of contradictions where I want to serve God with all my heart and mind, but am pulled by the influence of sin to do something totally different (Romans 7:24–25 MSG).

The Standard Against Sin

The Ten Commandments are a crucial part of God's covenant with the human race, and they still provide the standard against sin and the foundation for many of the legal systems in the modern world. They appear twice in the Old Testament, in Exodus 20 and Deuteronomy 5, in this order:

1. You shall have no other gods before the Lord God.
2. You shall not make for yourself a carved image, or any likeness of anything that is in heaven above or earth beneath. You shall not bow down to them and serve them.
3. You shall not take the Lord's name in vain.
4. You shall remember the Sabbath day, to keep it holy.
5. You shall honor your mother and father.
6. You shall not murder.
7. You shall not commit adultery.
8. You shall not steal.
9. You shall not bear false witness against your neighbor.
10. You shall not covet.

These principles relate to right behavior and worship in life and society, and they still remain the foundation for conduct in many nations today.

Jesus confirmed the importance of the Ten Commandments in the New Testament, and then He explained that God always looks *beyond* outward rule-keeping to examine our individual thoughts and heart motives (see Matthew 5:17–22).

James described our sin situation this way:

You're cheating on God. If all you want is your own way, flirting with the world every chance you get, you end up enemies of God and his way. And do you suppose God doesn't care? The proverb has it that "he's a fiercely jealous lover." And what he gives in love is far better than anything else you'll find. It's common knowledge that "God goes against the willful proud; God gives grace to the willing humble" (James 4:4–6 MSG).

The devil, our common enemy, wants us to break God's commandments. He comes at us as individuals, families, communities and even nations. He is persistent and skilled at deception and persuasion, but always remember that *he isn't all-powerful.* He was defeated, thrown out of heaven and humiliated by Jesus, the Lord of Lords and King of Kings.

Jesus said, "The thief [referring to Satan] does not come, except to steal and kill and destroy. I came that they may have life, and that they may have it more abundantly" (John 10:10 MEV). Jesus is more than enough for us in every situation.

Sin can steal your job, marriage and family, and ultimately it may steal your very soul.

On May 25, 2020, cell phone footage of the brutal death of George Floyd shocked the world. Four police officers participated in the inhumane arrest and treatment of Mr. Floyd. However, the fatal actions of Officer Derek Chauvin sparked national and global protests against police brutality, especially toward people of color.

Mr. Floyd said three last words as he lay dying on the pavement with Chauvin's knee on his neck: "I can't breathe." Those words will forever ring out against unchecked sins of racism, brutality and uncontrolled anger.

George Floyd's life ended violently that day in May of 2020. He can no longer care for his daughter or interact with his family. The lives of Derek Chauvin and the three other officers changed forever as well.

Those former police officers will never again receive respect as the "men in blue" from the City of Minneapolis. Citizens and even other members of law enforcement look down on them.

A *New York Times* article said it took the racially diverse jury only ten hours to convict Chauvin on all three charges—second-degree murder, third-degree murder and second-degree manslaughter.[7]

The judge in the case later sentenced Chauvin to 22½ years in prison. The other three officers were convicted of violating Mr. Floyd's civil rights.

The actions of one man, Derek Chauvin, negatively affected the lives of many in this tragic case.

The Ultimate Impact of Sin

The soul is the most precious thing you will ever have. How you live and the choices you make determine your life after death. Again, the ultimate impact of sin is to rob you of eternal life with God. It separates you from God with everlasting punishment in hell.

Jesus described sin's effect in the life of one rich man in particular.

There was a rich man who was clothed in purple and fine linen and who feasted sumptuously every day. And at his gate was laid a poor man named Lazarus, covered with sores, who desired to be fed with what fell from the rich man's table. Moreover, even the dogs came and licked his sores. The poor man died and was carried by the angels to Abraham's side. The rich man also died and was buried, and in Hades, being in torment, he lifted up his eyes and saw Abraham far off and Lazarus at his side (Luke 16:19–23 ESV).

Then Jesus described the rich man's concern that his brothers would follow in his footsteps and end up in the same place.

> And he said, "Then I beg you, father [Abraham], to send him [Lazarus] to my father's house—for I have five brothers—so that he may warn them, lest they also come into this place of torment" (Luke 16:27–28 ESV).

Life does not depend on the type of job you have, the market value of your home, or the kind of car you drive.

The practice of sin robs you of true and lasting joy in life now and forever because there is no real joy in life apart from God. Sin separates you from God.

Sin, left unchecked, will rob you of your soul.

So the next time you choose to sin, think about your soul and who else will be impacted by that choice. Remember that sin can have *generational impact*. Do you really want your children and grandchildren to get caught up years from now in your bad decision today?

The Holy Spirit is saying, "Master sin. Overcome it!"

Chapter Two

Cain vs. Abel:
Anger, Excuses and Homicide

The sin that Adam and Eve committed in the Garden evidently affected their firstborn son, Cain, and later produced tragic results for their second child, Abel. Although Abel had the same physical DNA and spiritual environment as Cain, he made better choices that led to very different outcomes.

> Time passed. Cain brought an offering to God *from the produce* of his farm. Abel also brought an offering, *but from the firstborn* animals of his herd, *choice cuts* of meat. God liked Abel and his offering, but Cain and his offering didn't get his approval. Cain lost his temper and went into a sulk (Genesis 4:3–5 MSG, italics mine).

Cain didn't understand that in order for his offering to be accepted by God, he himself had to be accepted. Cain was not accepted because of his sin. The giving of his offering became a moment of revelation, exposing the true motives of the heart (and it still is in our day).

Sin contaminated Cain's worship. His wrong choices ultimately led to a deadly plot and a lifelong curse. His story resonates with the divine warning echoed in this book: "Master sin, or sin will master you!"

Cain was a farmer and Abel was a shepherd. Both men had honorable vocations that produced things of value to give to God as part of their worship. The sin that separated Cain wasn't rooted in his gift; *it was in his heart*.

All Are Gifted of God

God gives gifts according to His purposes and assignments for us on earth. The natural talents, abilities and spiritual giftings He provides help us to make the world a better place and equip us to represent Him during our time on earth.

When God gives you a gift, trust that He does not give cheaply. He never gives degraded or secondhand gifts that are less than His best.

James, the apostle, assured us that "every good gift and every perfect gift is from above, coming down from the Father of lights, with whom there is no variation or shadow due to change" (James 1:17 ESV).

To be clear, Cain and Abel each received good and perfect gifts, but they displayed different heart attitudes toward true worship of God. True worship is a giving of one's self to God, not just an "offering." We must love the Lord with all our hearts and our neighbors as ourselves. (See Matthew 22:36–39.)

Cain's problems only got worse after the Lord rejected his offering because his contaminated-heart attitude exploded in emotional turmoil and self-pity.

Cain's Anger and the Danger of Sin at the Door

The LORD said to Cain, "Why are you angry? Why is your countenance fallen? If you do well, shall

you not be accepted? But if you do not do well, sin
is crouching at the door. It desires to dominate you,
but you must rule over it" (Genesis 4:6–7 MEV).

This passage takes us directly to the heart of Cain's problem (and ours as well). The Lord moves past Cain's outward religious actions with a straightforward question. In essence, He asks, "Can you explain why you are angry, Cain?" Sin was the core root of Cain's problem.

James, the apostle, asks a similar question and then answers it.

Where do you think all these appalling wars and
quarrels come from? Do you think they just happen? Think again. They come about because
you want your own way, and fight for it deep in-
side yourselves. You lust for what you don't have
and are willing to kill to get it. *You want what isn't
yours* and will risk violence to get your hands on it
(James 4:1–2 MSG, italics mine).

Why does James focus on "you" rather than refer to "they," "them" or "somebody else"? Parents, friends and circumstances can and do influence us to sin. Yet, each of us must accept personal responsibility for our choices, lay aside blame and stand *on our own* before God.

**To hide and excuse our sin may "be human,"
but we defeat sin as we admit our sins, take
responsibility for them and correct them through
God's grace and power of the Holy Spirit.**

God asked Cain, "Why are you angry? Why is your countenance fallen?" Cain reacted with extreme anger and became gloomy. The emotion of anger comes whether you welcome it or not, and the fact that something makes you angry doesn't make it a sin. The way you deal with that anger (and its source) makes the difference.

Apostle Paul urged the young Ephesian church to live in unity, seek maturity and to not conform to the fallen ways of the world. Should a situation arise that causes you to be angry, let it be as Christ's anger—without sin (see Mark 3:5). Anger at wrong is justifiable, but we must rule over it and release it before the day ends.

> "In your anger do not sin": Do not let the sun go down while you are still angry, and *do not give the devil a foothold* (Ephesians 4:26–27 NIV, italics mine).

Once you choose to cling to anger and nurture it in your heart, it becomes *sin*. Anger left unchecked in the heart only grows to produce ruin and chaos like a malignant cancer. Jesus said this:

> For from within, *out of the heart of men*, proceed evil thoughts, adultery, fornication, murder, theft, covetousness, wickedness, deceit, licentiousness, an evil eye, blasphemy, pride and foolishness (Mark 7:21–22 MEV, italics mine).

Angry people flood human society. They populate grocery store checkout lines, banks, fast food drive-through lanes, and virtually every major thoroughfare and highway of the world.

It seems that angry and confrontational voices dominate our digital social network streams. Why are there so many angry people? It is because of sin and the wounds it produces.

I'm convinced that we've passed down an anger addiction to our younger generations. Children lash out in unchecked anger at parents, teachers and each other in defiant, raging curses.

If you peel back the layers of blame and excuses, you find there is no reason for it other than sin. Again, the Bible describes this process in Cain's life with the phrase "his countenance fell" (Genesis 4:5 MEV). Anger took over; he had no joy.

It's About the Heart

God later reveals the key to Cain's failure and what he could do about it. We know from the Scriptures that the Lord loved Cain unconditionally. Cain didn't have to earn or regain God's love, but he had a responsibility to master the *sin* in his life by dealing with his attitude and values. This was about Cain's heart condition, and God warned him because He cared. It's worth examining again.

> God spoke to Cain: "Why this tantrum? Why the sulking? If you do well, won't you be accepted? And if you don't do well, sin is lying in wait for you, ready to pounce; it's out to get you, *you've got to master it*" (Genesis 4:6–7 MSG, italics mine).

From childhood forward, our sinful human nature may seem to work and "slip under the radar" with our parents, friends or employers. However, it definitely doesn't work with God.

The Lord's answer to Cain's condition still speaks to you and me today: "If you do well, won't you be accepted? And if you don't do well, sin is lying in wait for you, ready to pounce; it's out to get you, you've got to master it."

God loves everyone and wants to accept each of us, but He has standards for us to follow. The first and foremost requirement is that we repent of sin and receive His Son, Jesus, as Lord and Savior. Then we follow the guideline He gave in the beginning; "do the right thing, then you and your worship will be accepted."

Don't expect to just slide into heaven (or slide around on earth, either). Whoever tells you that God does not have standards is not telling the truth. Jesus made it clear that *no one*, absolutely no human, can keep all of the commandments in the Bible on his or her own.

> Therefore *no one will be declared righteous* in God's sight by the works of the law; rather, through the law we become conscious of our sin.
> But now apart from the law the righteousness of God has been made known, to which the Law and the Prophets testify. *This righteousness is given through faith in Jesus Christ* to all who believe. There is no difference between Jew and Gentile, *for all have sinned and fall short of the glory of God*, and all are *justified freely by his grace* through the redemption that came by Christ Jesus (Romans 3:20–24 NIV, italics mine).

Why did the Lord tell Cain, "And if you don't do well, sin is lying in wait for you, ready to pounce; it's out to get you, *you've got to master it*" in Genesis 4:7 (MSG)? He said it *because it is true*. It was Cain's wrong choices that led to the first homicide recorded in the Bible.

The "nature of the heart" matters to God! The Bible makes it clear that the Lord always looks beyond our outward gifts, offerings and religious actions to gauge the inward thoughts and intents of the heart.

When the Bible speaks of sin "lying in wait" and ready to "pounce," it reminds us of the apostle Peter's warning. (Remember, this man was the most hotheaded and impulsive member of Jesus's inner circle at one time.)

Keep a cool head. Stay alert. *The Devil is poised to pounce, and would like nothing better than to catch you napping.* Keep your guard up. You're not the only ones plunged into these hard times. It's the same with Christians all over the world. So keep a firm grip on the faith. The suffering won't last forever. It won't be long before this generous God who has great plans for us in Christ— eternal and glorious plans they are!—will have you put together and on your feet for good. He gets the last word; yes, he does (1 Peter 5:8–11 MSG, italics mine).

A lion *crouches* in a hidden place before it *pounces* for the kill. If you play with sin too long, the enemy will get you because he is ready and eager to pounce on any unsuspecting prey.

Sin doesn't care how old or how young you are. It doesn't care about the color of your skin or what part of the world you live in. God told Cain, "Sin is crouching at your door—it is lying in wait for you—and its desire is for you."

God goes on to tell Cain, "You must master sin." What follows is as old as Adam and Eve. It shows up with the first false excuse recorded in Bible history!

When God finds Adam and Eve hiding among the trees in the Garden of Eden, He confronts them—and out comes the first string of humanity's excuses:

But the Lord God called to the man, "Where are you?"

He answered, "I heard you in the garden, and I was afraid because I was naked; so I hid."

And he said, "Who told you that you were naked? Have you eaten from the tree that I commanded you not to eat from?"

> The man said, "*The woman you put here with me*—she gave me some fruit from the tree, and I ate it."
> Then the LORD God said to the woman, "What is this you have done?"
> The woman said, "*The serpent deceived me, and I ate*" (Genesis 3:9–13 NIV, italics mine).

This "sound loop" of excuses simply replays over and over again from generation to generation with ever-decreasing truth or reality.

"But I can't quit it, Lord. You know how it is. I mean, I try. I really do try. I go to church on Sundays, and I stop for a little while, but then…."

We must master it. God has already done His part. Jesus meant what He said at the end of it all, just before He died. He said, "It is finished" (John 19:30b).

We want God to do everything, but Jesus has done everything that needs to be done for us.

Yes, He hears every prayer and still answers prayer, but the "heavy lifting" was all done when Jesus endured the beatings and the thirty-nine stripes of the whip. He completed it when He died on the cross, rose again and was seated in heaven at the right hand of the Father.

The Bible says that God "had regard for Abel and his offering; but for Cain and his offering He had no regard" (Genesis 4:4–5 NASB). Perhaps Cain tainted his offering with a wrong motive (such as jealousy) or a wrong attitude (such as pride—he was the firstborn, after all).

The Bible speaks prophetically about vain worship versus the real deal, and Jesus Himself confirms the warnings:

> The Lord says: "These people come near to me with their mouth and honor me with their lips, *but*

their hearts are far from me. Their worship of me is based on merely human rules they have been taught" (Isaiah 29:13 NIV, italics mine).[1]

Yet a time is coming and has now come when the true worshipers will worship the Father in the Spirit and in truth, for they are the kind of worshipers the Father seeks. God is spirit, and his worshipers must worship in the Spirit and in truth" (John 4:23–24 NIV).

God Searches for True Worshipers

You *are* your offering, just as you *are* your word. Some people say, "You are whatever you say. Your word is your bond. That's how I know you—by your word. If you don't fulfill your word, then you are no good."

There is truth in these statements.

Your offering to God is tied directly to you. If you offer God something halfheartedly, then both the gift and the giver are halfhearted. I suspect that this was Cain's problem—the giver was halfhearted, so he tainted his gift as well and both were rejected.

Don't serve God halfheartedly. You *are* your gift. If you want to offer God something, then give Him your best.

You also should give the people around you your best. You are the only "Bible" some of your coworkers, associates or classmates may ever see. They may never hear a sermon or read the Gospels in their lifetime if they don't see Jesus in you and your actions first!

I'm concerned that many of us who go to church every week may end up with worship and service *that God doesn't (and can't) accept.* There are many rich and beneficial rituals, worship styles and lifestyles of faith in the Christian world— but *all require a heart and life* filled with love, gratitude, faith and obedience to Christ.

Chapter Three

Am I My Brother's Keeper?
The Case for Unity

Now Cain said to his brother Abel, "Let's go out to the field." While they were in the field, Cain attacked his brother Abel and killed him.

Then the LORD said to Cain, "Where is your brother Abel?"

"I don't know," he replied. *"Am I my brother's keeper?"* (Genesis 4:8–9 NIV, italics mine).

God created us as complex, multi-layered creatures. Sin begins in the heart and then works itself out through our human emotions and actions.

This helps explain why sin is so deeply rooted in our lives—it resembles metastatic cancer in the way it can invade and destroy virtually every area of our lives if left unchecked.

No good comes from willful ignorance or blindness to sin. When God called out Cain over his sin and the homicide it produced, Cain deflected personal responsibility with mock ignorance. He simply wasn't prepared for its severe consequences (and neither are we).

And then He said, "What have you done? The voice of your brother's blood is crying out to Me from the ground. Now *you are cursed from the ground* which opened its mouth to receive your brother's blood from your hand. From now on when you till the ground, it will not yield for you its best. You will be a fugitive and a wanderer on the earth."

Then Cain said to the LORD, "*My punishment is more than I can bear.* You have driven me out this day from the face of the earth, and from your face will I be hidden; and I will be a fugitive and a vagabond in the earth, and it will happen that anyone who finds me will kill me" (Genesis 4:10–14 MEV, italics mine).

Cain and Abel shared at least one part of their purpose: they each were to freely give back to God a portion of His gift to them. We share this part in our own lives as well.

It is foolish to reject or oppose your God-given purpose when your divine design can actually "bend" you toward that purpose from childhood. It is equally foolish to demand that other people "bend" themselves in *your* direction when they are responsible to follow their own divine design and purpose.

Division and strife over our differences remain some of the greatest sins of the human race. Differences in theology have been used to justify brutal persecution, imprisonment, torture and homicide!

God wants His family to live and work together in unity. Unity is so important that two of Jesus's most striking statements feature its importance:

1. He said that *His disciples would be known by their love for one another* (paraphrased from John 13:34–35). He

meant it. He *still* expects to see this love set you and I apart from the world.

2. He also issued a solemn warning about what happens *in the absence of unity*: "If a house is divided against itself, that house cannot stand" (Mark 3:25 NIV). What does that say about our splintered and divided church today?

Get out of the Blame Game and Take Responsibility

God loves us so much that He confronts us when sin is "at the door" of our lives and has entered in. We see it clearly in Cain's life.

> And then [God] said, "What have *you* done? The voice of your brother's blood is crying out to Me from the ground. Now you are cursed from the ground which opened its mouth to receive your brother's blood from your hand. From now on when you till the ground, it will not yield for you its best. You will be a fugitive and a wanderer on the earth" (Genesis 4:10–12 MEV, italics mine).

In typical human fashion, Cain immediately blames God for the painful consequences of his own choices and actions.

> Then Cain said to the LORD, "My punishment is more than I can bear. *You* have driven me out this day from the face of the earth, and from your face will I be hidden; and I will be a fugitive and a vagabond in the earth, and it will happen that anyone who finds me will kill me" (Genesis 4:13–14 MEV, italics mine).

How often are we tempted to blame God, friends, enemies or *anyone other than* ourselves for wrong choices and actions in life? Then the memorized excuses kick in: "Well, that's just human nature." Perhaps.

Neither false blame nor excuses are part of God's nature. Nor should we tolerate the "blame game" or excuses in our lives—even if we deal with people who "deserve" to be blamed.

The Scriptures imply that Cain planned his evil act. He premeditated and plotted to entice his brother to an isolated field away from every witness (or so he thought). He ignored every warning and his inner sense of right and wrong to pursue his desire and rage against his brother. Ultimately, Cain committed cold-blooded murder and tried to avoid accepting responsibility for his deed to God's face.

Sin leads to more sin, more deception, and, in Cain's case, more lies to cover itself and to escape ever-growing consequences.

If God put Cain on trial in a modern Western court, he would be convicted of first-degree murder—a finding that requires proof of premeditation and planning. If you did it, if you plotted it, if you premeditated it, it's first-degree murder.

God, the just judge, told Cain, "...you are cursed from the ground which opened its mouth to receive your brother's blood from your hand." If God curses you, you are cursed.

Man can say you are cursed all day long and that won't amount to anything. If the Lord says you are cursed, however, then you are.

In light of Jesus's victory on the cross, if Cain had repented of his sin, then he would have been forgiven. Yet God showed His love for him.

> So the LORD said to him, "Therefore whoever kills Cain, vengeance will be taken on him sevenfold." Then the LORD put a mark upon Cain, so that no one finding him would kill him. Then Cain went out from the presence of the LORD and settled in the land of Nod, east of Eden (Genesis 4:15–16 MEV).

The "excuse game" is painfully familiar to every parent, counselor, psychologist, wife, husband, child or friend who has tried to help or live with someone who has an addiction. "But you know I have this craving. Uh, you know, I got past three o'clock, but then it just overtook me."

When we use blame-laying and excuses to disguise and cover our sin, we empower sin to devour more of our lives.

James, the apostle, has a better way for us:

So let God work his will in you. Yell a loud *no* to the Devil and watch him make himself scarce. Say a quiet *yes* to God and he'll be there in no time. Quit dabbling in sin. Purify your inner life. Quit playing the field. Hit bottom, and cry your eyes out. The fun and games are over. Get serious, really serious. Get down on your knees before the Master; it's the only way you'll get on your feet (James 4:7–10 MSG).

Back out of your sin and you will master it. Even if you fall, get up again! Don't continue to go that route.

Very few victories come with a single knockout blow. You master sin by getting up again after you are knocked down. Sometimes you master sin by confronting and turning away. At other times you win a battle by running away (from sexual sin, for instance).

So flee youthful desires and pursue righteousness, faith, love, and peace, with those who call on the Lord out of a pure heart (2 Timothy 2:22 MEV).

As disciples following Jesus in a fallen world, we overcome by starting over again. We can't afford to give in to the pressure of our mistakes, shortcomings or the noisy people hoping and cheering for our failure.

God promised us in Proverbs 24:16, "Indeed a righteous person will fall seven times, and *then get up again*, but the guilty will collapse in calamity" (NET, italics mine).

Get up in faith and keep going:

"I'm back in the fight, Lord. I must overcome. I've got to get over it. I might have fallen then, but it's okay. I am going to push it back tomorrow.

"I messed up again, Lord. Please forgive me. With Your help, I'll start over, and I'm going to conquer it."

Wandering Without Purpose

Many people suffer needlessly because they live their lives wandering "outside" of God. They may have an address and live in a house, but they are wanderers with no sense of purpose or direction.

"Oh, but I get up and go to work every day."

Yes, you get up and work a job you don't even enjoy. The truth is that you have no real joy, no real life and no real sense of purpose. You wake up and start your day, but you can't wait until it ends so you can go to sleep at night.

If we avoid God and wander through life in our sin with no sense of purpose or direction, then the only reward for our choice is a cursed life.

Cain chose anger and violence, and then he complained to the Lord that his punishment was "too great to bear" in Genesis 4:13. He failed to recognize something his parents before him failed to see as well: the promise to be like God or to be the "dominant" one looks good on the front side, but it delivers hellish separation and brokenness on the back side. The devil makes great promises but never lets us see the end result or consequence of sin.

The enemy of our souls blinds us with false visions and deafens us with the things we want to hear—all to prevent our realization that we won't be able to bear the outcome or deal with the consequences of our wrong choices.

Those consequences can really change God's plan for us by sending us in a different direction, thereby causing us to miss our appointed time and purpose. The outcome of sin is a curse.

God has blessed each of us with individual gifts and talents. Some of us can cook well while others can sew, build massive skyscrapers, teach, design aircraft or navigate the high seas.

Since these talents and abilities are usually tied closely to our purpose in life, we should learn how God intends for us to *help each other* with our different gifts. You may be strong in an area where I am not. I may excel at things you do not. What if we helped one another reach our goals?

Many of us mimic Cain's sarcastic answer when we hear the call to help others: "Am I my brother's keeper?" Perhaps we should follow in the footsteps of Jesus, who loved us so much that He willingly stepped down from His throne and sacrificed Himself on the cross to save us and give us a new life (see John 3:16 and Luke 19:10).

Since childhood I've loved to study, while most of the children growing up around me hated it. This natural "bent" exposed me early on to a fundamental problem in the human condition—the sin of jealousy.

I still hear it at times: "You're always studying. When are you going to stop going to school?" I typically answer, "When I get to heaven."

The Lord "bent" me toward study, learning and analysis. I like to study. Many people endure taunts in their school years labeling them as "nerds," "bookworms," "religious 'goody-two-shoes'" or "science geeks."

I say, how dare we try to downgrade the "bent" or giftings of others? The world is filled with stories of overcomers from this group who go on to brilliant careers producing new medicines, inventions and scientific breakthroughs that save or enrich the lives of the very people who mocked them earlier.

Cain actually did well in the beginning. He was a good farmer, and he brought his produce as an offering to God. Sadly, Cain failed to understand that the state of his heart and his attitude directly affected the quality of his gifts and how God reacted toward the giver.

He evidently chose his gifts as if he were gathering produce for a public market. He should have chosen his gifts as if they were being given to the most powerful and important person in the known world.

He didn't. When God rejected Cain's offering and explained why, Cain became angry, blamed God and took out his jealous rage on his brother.

Cain's "victim rant" may reveal some reasons we need to avoid sin and its victim mentality in our own lives.

First, he accused God of driving him "from the face of the earth" (Genesis 4:14 MEV). He, like his parents before him, pointedly ignored God's direct warnings. Adam and Eve were driven from the Garden of God and the potential eternal life they were designed for. Cain's evil choice dictated the nature of its consequence: the earth itself rejected him after he spilled his own brother's blood onto soil that had never "tasted" human blood before.

Cain's second complaint was far more serious. He said, "… and from your face will I be hidden" (Genesis 4:14 MEV). He was saying, "I will be hidden from You. I won't be able to have access to You."

If Cain had repented instead of deflecting, hiding his sin and blaming God, then he would have been forgiven. Sadly, the devil's greatest trick is to convince us that we can hold onto sin and also retain our access to God. No, the only divine access you and I have in this life of struggle is through genuine repentance.

Always remember that God loves you—even when you sin. He just doesn't want you to stay there. If you don't believe me, then believe His Word.

> But go and learn what this means, "I desire mercy, and not sacrifice." For I [Jesus] have not come to call the righteous, but sinners, to repentance (Matthew 9:13 MEV).

> But God demonstrates His own love toward us, in that while we were yet sinners, Christ died for us (Romans 5:8 MEV).

> This is a faithful saying and worthy of all acceptance, that Christ Jesus came into the world to save sinners, of whom I [Paul] am the worst (1 Timothy 1:15 MEV).

God loves us all the time and wherever we stand with Him, but He hates sin and wants us to master it. The Bible says that after his conversation with God, Cain *"went out from the presence of the LORD and settled in the land of Nod"* (Genesis 4:16 MEV, italics mine).

The word *Nod* means "wandering place."[1] In other words, Cain left God's presence and settled in "no man's land." Any place separated from God is dead; it is a place of wandering. I don't know about you, but I don't want to wander. I want to know where I am going and how to get there.

Do you feel as if you are wandering around with no sense of direction or purpose for your life? You need to know God's purpose for your life so you can fulfill it. The first thing to do is to get rid of sin in your life.

Stop ignoring sin; start mastering it today. Identify anything or any actions that violate the Word of God. As Paul said:

> …lay aside every weight and the sin that so easily entangles us, and let us run with endurance the race that is set before us (Hebrews 12:1 MEV).

Chapter Four

How to Overcome Sin

There is hope. The book of Romans describes the supernatural power God released on our behalf, and *The Message* version seems to capture its dynamic nature. Our challenge is to hear, trust and run our race in life with confidence.

> With the arrival of Jesus, the Messiah, that fateful dilemma [of wanting to do good, but doing evil instead] is resolved. Those who enter into Christ's being-here-for-us no longer have to live under a continuous, low-lying black cloud. A new power is in operation. The Spirit of life in Christ, like a strong wind, has magnificently cleared the air, freeing you from a fated lifetime of brutal tyranny at the hands of sin and death (Romans 8:1–2 MSG).

Sin destroys, so you and I have to master it. You have the power within you because God made you after His likeness and in His image. He has given you power and the gift of self-control by His Spirit. You can do it. Yes, you can.

We recognize the apostle Peter today as much for his human failings as for his courage and faith. He was hot-tempered, impulsive and sometimes seemed addicted to the approval of other people. Peter was the one disciple who publicly denied Jesus three times on the night He was betrayed. That makes the words he wrote later in his life even more powerful for us today:

> Grace and peace be yours in abundance through the knowledge of God and of Jesus our Lord.
> *His divine power has given us everything we need for a godly life through our knowledge of him* who called us by his own glory and goodness. Through these he has given us his very great and precious promises, so that through them you may participate in the divine nature, having escaped the corruption in the world caused by evil desires (2 Peter 1:2–4 NIV, italics mine).

Jesus overcame every power opposing us. He broke every chain that seeks to bind us, but we can't afford to be ignorant about strongholds (areas in our lives or family history where evil influences seem especially strong).

Acknowledge the tough situations and challenges in your life, but stand strong in your trust that God is at work in *every* area of your life.

Let's again read through some extremely practical advice from James, the apostle, in his down-to-earth letter to the Church:

> So let God work his will in you. Yell a loud *no* to the Devil and watch him make himself scarce. Say a quiet *yes* to God and he'll be there in no time. Quit

dabbling in sin. Purify your inner life. Quit playing the field. Hit bottom, and cry your eyes out. The fun and games are over. Get serious, really serious. Get down on your knees before the Master; it's the only way you'll get on your feet (James 4:7–10 MSG).

Cain *heard* God's message but *chose* to ignore it. Yielding to jealousy, he chose anger over divine wisdom. Don't be like Cain. His burning jealousy fed his anger.

Solomon said, "Set me as a seal upon thine heart, as a seal upon thine arm: for love is strong as death; *jealousy is cruel as the grave*: the coals thereof are coals of fire, which hath a most vehement flame" (Song of Solomon 8:6 KJV, italics mine).

If Cain's life is any indicator, it means the sin of jealousy can kill. It will murder if it isn't mastered.

The strife between Cain and Abel is the first earthly evidence that just because people have the same blood flowing in their veins doesn't mean they have the same love for one another.

It is just as serious in the spiritual family of God, where people who each claim salvation under the name of Jesus end up acting very *unlike* Him in their jealousy and anger toward each other.

The Choices That Face Us

According to the 2020 U.S. Census, African Americans and those who identify as Black "in combination" with another race comprise 14.2 percent of the total population. Yet this population was victimized by 32.7 percent of all the violent crimes and 54.4 percent of all the homicides committed in the nation.[1]

A commentary article on crime and justice published by *The Daily Signal* (of The Heritage Foundation), noted that the

FBI's National Incident-Based Reporting System (NIRS) statistics indicate *the total percentage of Black offenders convicted of homicide in 2020 had reached 54.7 percent in the nation.*[2]

The authors, GianCarlo Canaparo and Abby Kassal, said:

> The increase in black offenders and black victims is reminiscent of the fallout from the Black Power movements of the 1960s. Historian C. Vann Woodward recounts that history in his magisterial book *"The Strange Career of Jim Crow."*[3]

Dr. C. Vann Woodward, winner of a Pulitzer Prize and a professor at Johns Hopkins University and Yale University, strongly supported many of the leaders of the Civil Rights Movement, including W.E.B. DuBois and Dr. Martin Luther King, Jr. In fact, Dr. Woodward's book "became part of a revolution as, in Martin Luther King, Jr.'s words, it became 'the historical Bible of the civil rights movement.'"[4]

Canaparo and Kassal continue:

> Woodward observed that radicals began to reject the approach of "the old civil rights movements," which called for peace, equality, and integration. The radicals favored "racial separatism" and "black nationalism," which gave way to "bursts of black violence, disorder, and frustration." The irony of this violence, however, was that it occurred primarily in black neighborhoods, and "the main victims" were working-class black people.[5]

They compared then with now when they concluded, "As with the riots of the 1960s, the anti-police riots of 2020 caused significant harm to black neighborhoods and black-owned businesses."[6]

We need to seek *more* than emotional expression of our pain. We need to *unify*, taking the holistic approach that embraces the spiritual, social and economic solution. We must help those in our communities who feel trapped in their situations—offering practical as well as spiritual support.

As an example, amazing things can happen when churches, government, businesses and nonprofits *in those communities* step up and come together to assist and lift those struggling to thrive in life.

Through it all, I am determined to keep my eyes on the One who is our solution, model and answer in this life and the next.

We can keep wasting time and generations trying to get *other* people to change their attitudes and actions. Or we can see ourselves as God sees us, overcome the obstacles set in our way, and take on the power and privileges He offers to us as sons and daughters of the Kingdom of God.

Choices matter. You and I have control over our choices. Choose wisely.

In the final analysis, it is *our* decision. We can choose unity or we can choose division and strife. We can hear and obey God, or we can hear and ignore Him. However, once we decide and act, the consequences are out of our hands.

If experience tells us that *"just because you have the same blood doesn't mean you have the same love,"* then we should make the kind of choices that foster and strengthen love and unity—in the family, church, community and world.

The Bible warns us that in the last days "…because lawlessness [sin] is increased, most people's love will become cold" (Matthew 24:12 NASB).

God is calling for family, friends and communities to have a hot love, a strong love, a love that is not easily shaken or moved, a love that goes deep and long. This "God kind of love" will keep us when everything else passes away.

We must love one another and master our sin because whatever sin we allow to flourish can adversely impact the lives of innocent people around us. So let us make sure no one is crying because of our sin.

Discover the Truth *about How God Feels about You*

How do you think God reacts to you when you struggle with sin day in and day out? You don't have to guess or speculate, and you don't need a doctorate degree in theology to find the truth. Consider what Jesus, Himself, said in Matthew's Gospel:

> Come unto me, all ye that labour and are heavy laden, and I will give you rest.
> Take my yoke upon you, and learn of me; for I am meek and lowly in heart: and ye shall find rest unto your souls.
> For my yoke is easy, and my burden is light (Matthew 11:28–30 KJV).

If you stay with Satan, your way will be hard. You will carry heavy burdens, and you will carry them alone. As Cain discovered the hard way, "Momma can only lift so much, and Daddy can only make so much right."

There are some things no one can lift but Jesus. And He is waiting and ready to help. He is the one who will make your way easy and lighten your load. He is the one who will bring you through life's struggles and help you carry its heavy burdens. God cares for you.

However, God will not impose Himself on you or use some minister to "strong arm" you with shame. It always comes down to your choice. My role as a minister is simply to point to the open door of God's love, but it's your decision. The book of Romans puts it this way:

What then? shall we sin, because we are not under the law, but under grace? God forbid.

Know ye not, that to whom ye yield yourselves servants to obey, his servants ye are to whom ye obey; whether of sin unto death, or of obedience unto righteousness?

But God be thanked, that ye were the servants of sin, but ye have obeyed from the heart that form of doctrine which was delivered you.

Being then made free from sin, ye became the servants of righteousness (Romans 6:15–18 KJV).

You are made free, so master sin!

Chapter Five

What Now?
Run to Win!

If you want to follow Christ in this life, then "run to win," not merely to get by with minimum commitment. That goes for any area of life. Jesus lived the "all-in, all-the-way" life in ministry, in persecution and in death. If you follow Him, you must be willing to live with the same heart attitude and mind-set.

As you think about giving back to God a portion of what He has given you, resolve to do it wholeheartedly and joyfully. When you praise Him, do it wholeheartedly. When you serve Him by serving others, do it joyfully as if you are serving the Lord Himself.

Give Him your best with all of your strength, ability and focus. The Bible says that King David "danced before the LORD with all his might" (2 Samuel 6:14 KJV). He did this despite the open disapproval and jealousy of his wife, Michal. (Sometimes the greatest critics of your wholehearted worship and giving to God will be members of your own family. Remember, it happened to Abel.)

Lift your voice to God! Get loud on His behalf. Make every visit to your church a time to give God your best. When you praise Him, move past average and offer Him extravagant praise. The Bible calls this "high praise"!

You just might discover that when you cross over into high praise, you will praise your way out of or right through a situation you thought was impossible.

High praise honors God and will absolutely "run the devil out of your house"! As for me and my house, we will offer high praise unto the Lord!

Saints Sin but Do Not Practice Sin

Many Christians think that just because they ran to an altar and "got saved" in the past, they don't have to deal with sin anymore. The truth is that *every believer has to master sin* to go on to progressive sanctification.

When you get saved, you are regenerated and your spirit is made new. However, as you live in this world, you have to deal in this world and face challenging choices every day.

Since you are not perfected yet, then in the process of becoming more like Jesus, you inevitably sin when you fall or slip into wrong choices.

What then?

Learn to immediately repent and turn away from your wrong choices and sin. Don't be surprised when you fail in an area of temptation; just don't make it a "practice." Repent, accept the Lord's forgiveness and move forward from there.

Allow the Holy Spirit to keep cleansing and purifying you. When you hear God's Word, then *do* the Word—one choice at a time, one hour at a time, and one day at a time. This is how you begin to master sin.

We live in a time when boundaries, moral standards and traditional values are looked down on and challenged as old-fashioned, out of touch and ignorant. Our culture preaches at us from grade school through college and through virtually every media that "everything is relative and subject to change according to each person's viewpoint."

The Lukewarm Life

Some things actually *do* change with time (especially fashions and fickle cultural moral standards). Christians, however, must learn to see things from God's perspective and understand that some things are wrong in any age and culture and that sin must still be dealt with.

In the book of Revelation, the Lord warns the Church about the danger of "the lukewarm life." The lukewarm life demands continual compromise and waters down our godly witness to fit into and accommodate the godless world around us. Jesus said:

> To the angel of the church in Laodicea write:
>
> The Amen, the faithful and true Witness, the Origin of the creation of God, says this:
>
> "I know your deeds, that *you are neither cold nor hot*; I wish that you were cold or hot. So *because you are lukewarm*, and neither hot nor cold, I will vomit you out of My mouth. Because you say, 'I am rich, and have become wealthy, and have no need of anything,' and you do not know that you are wretched, miserable, poor, blind, and naked, I advise you to buy from Me gold refined by fire so that you may become rich, and white garments so that you may clothe yourself and the shame of your nakedness will not be revealed; and eye salve to apply to your eyes so that you may see. *Those whom I love, I rebuke and discipline*; therefore be zealous and repent. Behold, I stand at the door and knock; if anyone hears My voice and opens the door, I will come in to him

and will dine with him, and he with Me. The one who overcomes, I will grant to him to sit with Me on My throne, as I also overcame and sat with My Father on His throne. The one who has an ear, let him hear what the Spirit says to the churches" (Revelation 3:14–22 NASB, italics mine).

It seems that the modern church has made the lukewarm life its chief doctrine, evangelism tool and discipleship model!

Reach Out and Run!

The Lord hardly seems passive about His expectations for His children. He plainly tells us that He rebukes and disciplines those He loves. In stark contrast to the "lukewarm model," the apostle Paul suggests a different way, a way that a person saved from sin can bring God honor and offer a solid witness to a fallen world:

I'm not saying that I have this all together, that I have it made. But I am well on my way, *reaching out* for Christ, who has so wondrously reached out for me. Friends, don't get me wrong: By no means do I count myself an expert in all of this, but *I've got my eye on the goal*, where *God is beckoning us onward*—to Jesus. *I'm off and running*, and I'm not turning back (Philippians 3:12–14 MSG, italics mine).

I see nothing *passive* in Paul's words here! We might think this man could rest a little and relax. After all, look at what he had already accomplished! We might sit back, but not him; *he is reaching out*!

We complain about being distracted by life and by so many attractive alternatives, but Paul *keeps his eyes on his goal*.

We may think God sits back on His throne once we are saved. *Paul pictures God gesturing and calling him onward* as he follows Jesus.

Paul tells us he's *off and running,* determined not to turn back for any reason.

Are you ready to master sin in your life? Are you sick and tired of being tormented by past failures or guilt?

1. Reach out to Christ and all that He has for you!
2. Set your eyes on the goal to please God and follow His purpose for your life.
3. Ignore every distraction or discouragement (including every reference to past failures or demands to "measure up").
4. Realize that God Himself is watching and encouraging you onward right now!
5. Leave that entangling or "clinging sin"[1] in the dust. You are off and running to claim the prize of eternal life in Jesus.
6. Make up your mind that you will not turn back for any reason—including any setbacks, temporary failures or discouragement that comes your way.
7. Separate yourself from those who are not running to win.

I'll let the writer of the book of Romans have the final say in this book on how to master your sin:

So, what do you think? *With God on our side like this, how can we lose?* (Romans 8:31 MSG, italics mine).

Endnotes

Chapter One: Sin and Its Impact

1 Merriam-Webster.com Dictionary, s.v. "sin," accessed June 22, 2023, https://www.merriam-webster.com/dictionary/sin.

2 U.S. Department of Justice-Federal Bureau of Investigation: 2019 Crime in the United States, accessed March 17, 2023, https://ucr.fbi.gov/crime-in-the-u.s/2019/crime-in-the-u.s.-2019/topic-pages/expanded-offense. The statistics are summarized here: file:///C:/Users/write/Downloads/FBI%20%E2%80%94%20Expanded%20Homicide.html.

3 Ibid. These specific statistics are taken from the written summary of a bar graph and pie chart entitled, "Murder by Relationship" in the statistics summary.

4 Ibid.

5 Ibid.

6 Ibid.

7 Tim Arango, Shaila Dewan, John Eligon and Nicholas Bogel-Burroughs, "Derek Chauvin is found guilty of murdering George Floyd," *New York Times,* April 20, 2021, updated June 25, 2021, https://www.nytimes.com/2021/04/20/us/chauvin-guilty-murder-george-floyd.html.

Chapter Two: Cain vs. Abel: Anger, Excuses and Homicide
1 This passage is also quoted in Ezekiel 33:31 and Matthew 15:7–9.

Chapter Three: Am I My Brother's Keeper? The Case for Unity
1 Strong's H5113 Nod = "wandering" – land to which Cain fled or wandered after the murder of Abel. H5113 - nôd - Strong's Hebrew Lexicon (KJV). Retrieved from https://www.blueletterbible.org/lexicon/h5113/kjv/wlc/0-1/.

Chapter Four: How to Overcome Sin
1 Nicholas Jones, Rachel Marks, Roberto Ramirez, Merarys Ríos-Vargas, "2020 Census Illuminates Racial and Ethnic Composition of the Country," August 12, 2021, updated June 10, 2022, https://www.census.gov/library/stories/2021/08/improved-race-ethnicity-measures-reveal-united-states-population-much-more-multiracial.html.

2 GianCarlo Canaparo and Abby Kassal, "Who Suffers the Most from Crime Wave?" *The Daily Signal*, April 12, 2022. https://www.dailysignal.com/2022/04/12/who-suffers-the-most-from-the-crime-wave/.

3 Ibid.

4 William S. McFeely, afterword of *The Strange Career of Jim Crow: Commemorative Edition* (New York: Oxford University Press, 2002), 221, as quoted in "Book Review: The Strange Career of Jim Crow 'Historical Bible of the Civil Rights Movement,'" The Smith Papers, accessed June 28, 2023, https://smith-papers.com/2022/07/11/book-review-the-strange-career-of-jim-crow-historical-bible-of-the-civil-rights-movement/.

5 Canaparo and Kassal, "Who Suffers the Most from Crime Wave?" *The Daily Signal*, April 12, 2022.

6 Ibid.

Chapter Five: What Now? Run to Win!

1 See Hebrews 12:1. A quick review of a sample of Bible translations reveals the lengths that these Bible translators take to describe the kind of sin we struggle with the most in this life; **the kind of sin that**: "*so readily (deftly and cleverly) clings to and entangles*" (AMPC), "*trips us up*" (NLT), "*just won't let go*" (CEV), "*so often makes us fall*" (ERV), "*distracts us*" (GW), "*holds on to us so tightly*" (GNT), "*so easily catches us*" (ICB), "[are] *parasitic sins*" (MSG), "*clings so closely*" (NET).

www.ingramcontent.com/pod-product-compliance
Lightning Source LLC
Chambersburg PA
CBHW061325120626
46546CB00007B/2678